Pebble® Plus

ALL ABOUT FALL

Apple Harvest

by Calvin Harris

Consulting Editor: Gail Saunders-Smith, PhD

Capstone press®

Mankato, Minnesota

Pebble Plus is published by Capstone Press,
151 Good Counsel Drive, P.O. Box 669, Mankato, Minnesota 56002.
www.capstonepress.com

1 2 3 4 5 6 12 11 10 09 08 07

Library of Congress Cataloging-in-Publication Data
Harris, Calvin, 1980–
    Apple harvest / by Calvin Harris.
    p. cm. —(Pebble plus. All about fall)
    Summary: "Simple text and photographs present an apple harvest in fall"—Provided by publisher.
    Includes bibliographical references and index.
    ISBN-13: 978-1-4296-0023-1 (hardcover)
    ISBN-10: 1-4296-0023-3 (hardcover)
    1. Apples—Harvesting—Juvenile literature. I. Title. II. Series.
SB363.H29 2008
634'.11—dc22   2006102053

Editorial Credits
Sarah L. Schuette, editor; Veronica Bianchini, designer; Charlene Deyle, photo researcher

Photo Credits
Capstone Press/Karon Dubke, 1, 5, 7, 9, 11, 13, 15, 17, 19
Corbis/James Marshall, 21
Shutterstock/MBWTE Photos, cover

Pebble Plus thanks Emma Krumbees in Belle Plaine, Minnesota and Sponsel's Minnesota Harvest in Jordan,
    Minnesota, for the use of their locations during photo shoots.

Note to Parents and Teachers

The All about Fall set supports national science standards related to changes during the
seasons. This book describes and illustrates the fall apple harvest. The images support
early readers in understanding the text. The repetition of words and phrases helps early
readers learn new words. This book also introduces early readers to subject-specific
vocabulary words, which are defined in the Glossary section. Early readers may need
assistance to read some words and to use the Table of Contents, Glossary, Read More,
Internet Sites, and Index sections of the book.

Table of Contents

Fall Is Here

It's fall.

Cool breezes blow through the apple orchard trees.

4

Red apples hang down
from the woody branches.

The ripe apples
are ready to be picked.
Fall is harvest time.

8

Picking Apples

Farmers pick the apples
by hand.

Workers sort the apples
by flavor.

The apples are put into bags
for shoppers to buy.

Haralson
$6.95
1/2 peck

13

Fun with Apples

Apples make fun treats.
Crisp caramel apples
are sticky and sweet.

Hot apple cider
warms you up
on a cold day.

Apple slices
fill the inside
of apple pies.

Other Signs of Fall

The apple harvest has begun.
What are other signs
that it's fall?

20

Glossary

breeze—a gentle wind

cider—a drink made by pressing the juice
out of apples

flavor—how something tastes

harvest—to gather or pick crops that are ripe

orchard—a field or farm where fruit trees grow;
some apple orchards have hundreds of trees.

ripe—ready to be picked or eaten

slice—a thin, flat piece cut from something larger

sort—to put into groups; apples are often sorted
by color and flavor.

Read More

Anderson, Catherine. *Apple Orchard.* Field Trip! Chicago: Heinemann, 2005.

Latta, Sara L. *What Happens in Fall?* I Like the Seasons. Berkeley Heights, N.J.: Enslow, 2006.

Mattern, Joanne. *How Apple Trees Grow.* How Plants Grow. Milwaukee: Weekly Reader Early Learning Library, 2006.

Internet Sites

FactHound offers a safe, fun way to find Internet sites related to this book. All of the sites on FactHound have been researched by our staff.

Here's how:

1. Visit *www.facthound.com*

2. Choose your grade level.

3. Type in this book ID **1429600233** for age-appropriate sites. You may also browse subjects by clicking on letters, or by clicking on pictures and words.

4. Click on the **Fetch It** button.

FactHound will fetch the best sites for you!

Index

Word Count: 93
Grade: 1
Early-Intervention Level: 12

24